"I started following Sara when she began posting her Daily Drives during the beginning of COVID on her Facebook page. I have experienced many leadership roles in the 34 years I have been a Realtor. I have also been a WW Coach for 13 years. Professionally, I relate to how helpful the tools she offers are, as well as, personally they are helping me improve how I interact with everyone I meet in my life's journey.

I highly recommend this book for everyone; as we can all learn from the journey we are taking with Sara's guidance."

- Carol Hesch,
Realtor, WW Coach

"I participated in an online training Sara gave on Living A Flourishing Life, and throughout my journey, I had so many breakthroughs. She has inspired me to transform as St. Paul calls us to in Rom 12:2 - 'Do not be conformed to this world, but be transformed by the renewal of your mind, that by testing you may discern what is the will of God, what is good and acceptable and perfect.'

What was even better is that her training and coaching provided me with some great tools with regards to learning about and assessing my well-being looking at the physical, community, career, social, and financial areas of well-being. We observed relationships with others, stopping along the journey, and exploring values. I had many discoveries about my self and continue to ponder putting them into practice at deeper and deeper levels. Thank you for offering Flourish!"

- Heather Sukut
Health Coach

"Sara Thingvold is a true example of someone who lives a flourishing life, and she has written her book with the same wisdom, dedication and respect that guides her life. Sara provides a roadmap that will enable you to live and model a life of well being. You will never regret taking this drive with Sara as you embark on your journey of living a flourishing life as well."

- Mark Deterding
Founder, Triune Leadership Services, LLC

"I have the pleasure and privilege of working with Sara Thingvold as a coach for our leadership development participants. Sara's deep understanding of the skills and qualities required to become servant leaders has been critical in supporting our employees in their professional development, but more importantly, I have a sincere respect for her compassionate approach. She genuinely cares about the success of everyone she works with, but also pushes them to achieve positive results."

- Pat Whitmore
Director of Human Resources
Prinsco, Water Management Solutions

"Sara is the queen of clarity.

When I struggle with difficult relationships or am tested by stressors I connect with Sara and receive her skilled, insightful assessment to determine what is really going on.

She unravels my confusion.

And I continue my journey through life renewed."

- Catherine Stine
The Stine Group

"Sara as my coach, has been instrumental in my growth as a leader – she has taught me the importance of composure, how I contribute and influence the workplace and of how my values play such a pivotal role in who I am as a leader. I am grateful for my time with her!"

- Brooke Zabel
Vice President of Human Resources, Knute Nelson

"It was in 2018 when Sara came to Titus 2 Ministry Center. Titus 2 Ministry works with women, and so I am used to talking with them. She intrigued me as she also was passionate about the scripture Titus 2:4. So we had coffee and talked. Little did I know how much she would impact my life. Titus 2 is a place where women help women to empower and strengthen them. Here is the journey I had with Sara. Over our many conversations, she was able to help me see where my cup was going empty. Doing a good thing is good, but it is doing. I had lost the focus of my self-care.

Sara was so patient with me. Leading me back to what I used to enjoy, "work" got the main priority. Although being a single mom, my focus was always on what needed to be done next and not myself. It is hard to change those mindsets and patterns of our life. I didn't know what I needed, but my soul was thirsting for this type of friendship. We worked through personal goals to the point where I now have a personal mission statement. I never thought I needed one just living life, but I did. What was my purpose, not just the employee, but who I am, and how do I ignite God's passions inside me again? I was trying to work with an empty cup, not knowing how to fill it up. I now can say because of this start back then and how our friendship has grown. She is one of the God-winks that come into your life, and I am so grateful she did. So many things I have learned from her. Thank You, Sara, for being you and doing and empowering those around you."

- Mary Yaw
Executive Director for Titus 2

To:

_____

From:

_____

LIVING A FLOURISHING —LIFE—

Daily Drive

A 12 DAY JOURNEY

SARA THINGVOLD

First Print Edition August 2020
ISBN 979-8-6630-3452-4

Book Cover and Formatting
www.uniquelytailored.com

SERVING SMARTER AT HOME AND WORK

www.sarathingvold.com

I dedicate this book to
Greg, Derrick, and Brooke Lynn,
my daily inspirations.

I am thankful and grateful to God, Jesus, and the Holy Spirit within me, granting me grace, hope, and love. Being strong with kindness because renewing my heart and my mind is essential in living a flourishing life for His glory.

- Sara

Life IS A Journey

Embrace and Enjoy the Drive!

How do you want to *be* (CWB)

How do you want to *feel* (CAF)

Your reason *how come* (BECAUSE)

CONTENTS

DAILY DRIVES:

How Come Extreme Self Care?

It's my pleasure to welcome you not just to a new servant leadership and self care book, but to a new lifestyle. I know changing the way you think, speak, feel, and act can be daunting. Self awareness is a continual learning process that I continue to practice every day. Keep in mind that this way of living life is not about what you cannot think, say, or do; it's about all of the ways your energy, relationships, and spirit will flourish and thrive.

My purpose in writing this book is to encourage and inspire you to appreciate and enjoy all the benefits of having a heart of peace, personally and professionally. This book offers three practical steps in your living a flourishing life within The Five Essential Elements of your Wellbeing. The Five Essential Elements are Career Wellbeing, Social Wellbeing, Financial Wellbeing, Physical Wellbeing, and Community Wellbeing.

It all begins by studying and understanding yourself, and watching and managing your patterns, similar to watching and managing the money in your banking and investment accounts. I can relate to overextending, burnout, loneliness, sadness, fear, anxiety, guilt and shame because I had been so busy trying to take care of and please others, personally and professionally, I found myself blaming others for my discontentment and frustrations. Even though I thought I was doing an okay job at work, reading, working out, eating well, and going to church, I was not taking good enough care of myself. In return, I was not serving others well. I was compromising my purpose, values, and integrity and did not have a heart at peace.

Extreme Self Care goes hand in hand with being a Servant Leader

Extreme Self Care is not easy. In order to serve others well, a person has to have a passion for personal development and taking care of themselves.

The word 'Extreme' in Extreme Self Care means to take a deeper dive, pausing consciously and competently, reflecting on your own personal and professional energy and spirit. It is not passive. It is not touchy feely. It is not optional. It is essential.

> *'A leader is a person who must take special responsibility for what's going on inside him or herself, inside his or her consciousness, lest the act of leadership create more harm than good.'*
>
> - Parker Palmer
> Leading From Within

> *'Only let each person lead the life that the Lord has assigned to him/her, and to which God has called them.'*
>
> -1 Corinthians 7:17

You are a Leader with a Leader's Heart

The truth about leading is that everyone is a leader. If you work full-time or part-time, volunteer, are an at home parent, or retired, every season of life and at every age, a person is a leader. A Leader is someone who consciously influences another person in what they think, feel, say, and do.

Join me on this road trip

This will be a short trip. Your road map includes exploring possibilities and opportunities; identifying the difference between big obstacles and small ones, helping decrease fears, anxiety, guilt, shame, loneliness, and sadness, while increasing your levels of joy, peace, and happiness.

A very special thank you to my mother who supported me and my writing along the way, editing material, championing, and encouraging me in the positive impact Daily Drives are making in the lives of others.
Thank you, Mom, I love you and value you.

Blessings in having a heart of peace and living a flourishing life!

Sara Thingvold
Ashby, MN
April 2020

Introduction

Daily Drive
Living a Flourishing Life

Contrary to what you think, your happiness is not rooted in your being happy. It is not rooted in your being healthy, wealthy, or wise. It is not rooted in your being an amazing athlete, physically healthy, or that your social status is within the top five percent of the community you live in or the community you spend time in on social media. What helps you be happy and live a flourishing life is consciously concentrating on how well you live out all Five of the Essential Elements interdependently instead of independently.

Every day you have a choice as to how you will live out that day. Nine out of ten decisions impact another person's decision. Many people wake up each morning on autopilot, with less than 2% of the world's population living with a purpose in mind. When your basic needs are not met you can feel sad, lonely, worthless, and afraid, depleting your wellbeing and mostly likely the wellbeing of others. Discerning your purpose, identifying your top five core values, and writing down a game plan, which is your vision of living out your purpose, has a transformational impact on your wellbeing and the wellbeing of others.

This began the birth of Daily Drives

Your decisions ripple six circles out, causing a domino effect into the world. Since most people live on autopilot not giving conscious thought to their purpose in life and in how their decisions impact others, developing self awareness is essential.

"Anger and resentment give short term gratification. Compassion and empathy breed long term satisfaction."
- Brooke Lynn Thingvold
Couple and Family Therapy, Graduate Student

3 Steps to Your Daily Drive

Daily Drive is a strategy, a faith based model and pivoting tool, offering direction with peace and harmony within The Five Essential Elements of your Wellbeing.

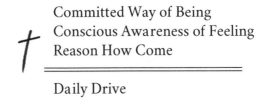

Committed Way of Being
Conscious Awareness of Feeling
Reason How Come
————————————————
Daily Drive

'The single biggest threat to your wellbeing is yourself. Without even giving it much thought, you allow your short-term decisions to override what's best for your long-term wellbeing.'
- Tom Rath and Jim Harter,
WELLBEING, the Five Essential Elements

Step 1: Committed Ways of Being, CWB

The state of being is the ability to act consciously competent within your mind, body, and spirit having a heart of peace and not a heart of war. It is radical, profound, and transformational.

I created a set of 9 Committed Ways of Being
   • Be Humble
   • Be Empathetic
   • Be Teachable
   • Be Respectful
   • Be Forgiving
   • Be Appreciative
   • Be Peaceful
   • Be Strong
   • Be Committed

Living life daily aligned with your purpose, behaving according to your core values, consciously competent with intentionality is not always easy. It has to be developed, learned, and practiced.

Step 2: Conscious Awareness of Feelings, CAF

Emotions are derivations of five core feelings: happiness, sadness, anger, fear, and shame. As you move through your daily routine - whether you're working, spending time with family or friends, eating, exercising, relaxing, or even sleeping - you are subject to a constant stream of emotions. It is so easy to forget that we have emotional reactions to almost everything that happens in our lives, whether we notice them or not. The complexity of these emotions is revealed in their varying forms of intensity."

- Travis Bradberry
EMOTIONAL INTELLIGENCE 2.0

Emotional Intelligence is being able to discriminate between different emotions and label them appropriately
• Awareness of the emotions within yourself
• Awareness of the emotions within others
• Managing the emotions within yourself
• Validating the emotions within others

Nine emotions to help you label and manage your emotions are:
- Love
- Joy
- Peace
- Patience
- Kindness
- Goodness
- Faithfulness
- Gentleness
- Self-Control

The third essential step in living a flourishing life intentionally is creating a reason for your being and feeling that certain way. I consider this third step the glue that ties your Committed Way of Being, CWB, and Conscious Awareness of Feeling, CAF, together. This step gives a boost of energy to your self awareness, which helps you have a heart of peace instead of a heart of war.

Step 3: Your Reason How Come, Because
Creating a reason gives additional clarity and focus in living a flourishing life with purpose and meaning.

Daily Drive example: Be Committed with Faithfulness Because everyone's lives matter.

When one person makes a positive change in managing their thoughts, feelings, words, and actions *it can have up to a 40% positive impact within their relationships.*

- The Gottman Institute

PAUSE

Think: What is your purpose for going through Daily Drives, what would you like to have happen in your life?

_____

Reflect: What goal would you like to create for yourself?

_____

Imagine: What will be the benefit for you if you do?

_____

What will be the benefit for others if you do?

_____

Practice: What can you do today to start?

_____

"...that according to the riches of his glory he may grant you to be strengthened with power through his Spirit in your inner being,"
-Ephesians 3:16

Let's Go For A Drive

CAREER WELLBEING
Managing what you think, feel, say, and do

> *"Engagement is an emotional commitment a person has for their work, the invisible force driving discretionary effort, and a reflection of the heart."*
> - Mark Miller
>
> *Take every thought captive.* - 2 Corinthians 10:5

Today, think about this:
Be humble with love because, one of the best opportunities for managing negative thoughts is by expressing gratitude.

- How do you awake and greet your day each morning?
- How confident are you in enjoying one thing you do every day?

Action Steps:

(Write or draw answers under Action Steps in Self Control section of your journal.)

First thing in the morning:

1. Give yourself and others a cheerful "Good Morning," smiling slightly from one side of your mouth or both.

2. Say one thing out loud that you are grateful for and looking forward to in your day.

3. Journal what will you do today that you enjoy, by yourself or with others, making certain you fully enjoy doing it.

Blessings to being humble with love, because a grateful heart builds energy towards having a heart at peace,
- Sara

Journal Example Page

If you are needing a more in-depth example of how to fill out these joual pages, please visit:

www.sarathingvold.com

to view a PDF that you can download and print at home. Just click **BOOK** in the menu bar and click on **DAILY DRIVE JOUNRAL EXAMPLE.**

Date: Day: Time:

PAUSE

Prepare | **A**cknowledge | **U**nderstand | **S**elf-Control | **E**ngage

---

Prepare

Read your Daily Drive

The Committed Way of Being, CWB

Circle the word 'Be' and circle how you are invited to 'Be' for today. *Example: **Daily Drive: Day One** (Be Humble)*

Conscious Awareness of Feeling, CAF

Circle the word 'with' and circle how you are invited to 'feel' for today. *Example: **Daily Drive: Day One** (with Love)*

The Reason 'How Come'

Draw a box around the word 'Because'.

Underline the words within the written Reason given for the day that stand out to you. *Example: **Daily Drive: Day One** | Because |*

*one of **the best opportunities to manage negative thoughts is** by expressing **gratitude**.*

Pause (Selah): Consciously connect within, being self-aware in attuning to your body's energy.

What tone are you currently sensing within your heart?

Circle: Peace | No Peace | Neutral | No Tension | Tension

Acknowledge

PRAY

"Lord, thank you for today, and thank you for placing your Holy Spirit within me helping me have a heart of peace in managing my thoughts, feelings, words, and actions."

God, strengthen me with power through Your Spirit in my inner being.
- Ephesians 3:16

Understanding

Reflect

- Consciously disconnect from any outlying distractions.

- Connect inward to your heart where the Holy Spirit resides.

- Connect your heart with your head, what is your head telling you about your heart:

_____

_____

- Identify or name the emotion(s) you are feeling:
(5 Core Emotions: 1. Sadness 2. Anger 3. Fear 4. Shame 5. Joy)

_____

Fill in the blanks:

Even Though I am feeling _____ it may cause tension within my heart and within my being, I am okay, God is with me.

I have every right to feel _____ it is not bad, it is normal, and God gives me the strength, endurance, and courage, to guard my heart with peace. I will get through this in time with His help.

Self-Control

Action Steps

Write or draw out your answer(s) to the question(s) from the Daily Drive today:

Write out your responses for each Drive's Action Step below, on index cards, or in a notebook:

_____

_____

_____

_____

_____

_____

Engage

1 2 3 4 5

Self-Awareness

On a scale of 1-5, rate yourself on how well you consciously and competently fulfilled the committed way of being, CWB, and conscious awareness of feeling, CAF, for the day and then write down your reason for how come, Because, you rated yourself how you rated yourself.

_____

_____

Close

Write 1-2 things you are taking away from the today's Daily Drive:

_____

_____

Write 1-2 things you can acknowledge yourself for from doing the today's Daily Drive:

_____

_____

Celebrate

- Say out loud:
  "I am thankful to God for my pursuing a heart of peace in living a flourishing life!"
- With a slight smile on one corner or both corners of your face.

'Living well is both a discipline and an art.'
- Sarah Young

CAREER WELLBEING
Managing what you think, feel, say, and do

> *"The men who succeed are the efficient few. They are the few who have the ambition and will power to develop themselves."*
> - Robert Burton

> *Guard your heart with all vigilance for from it flows the springs of life.*
> - Proverbs 4:23

Today, think about this:
Be empathetic with joy because, self awareness, pausing and turning inward, consciously understanding and regulating myself physiologically helps keep my mind, body, and spirit healthy; filled with joy and flourishing.

(Opportunity to journal now under Action Steps.)
- How do you give yourself permission to comfort yourself?
- How do you give yourself permission to comfort others?

Are you able to understand, value, and share the feelings of yourself and others?

Gallup defines Career Wellbeing as how you occupy your time or simply liking what you do every day. It is the first of the five essential elements in living a flourishing life. Whether a person works, volunteers, is a stay-at-home parent, or is retired, enjoying your day matters.

Research shows that those who stay focused and engaged in their day have significantly higher levels of happiness throughout their day. Those who are disengaged have stress levels that are substantially higher.

Those with a thriving Career Wellbeing live consciously engaged in their day with a deeper purpose in life and a plan to attain their goals.

Action Steps:
(Write or draw answers under Action Steps in Self Control section of your journal.)

1. Before getting out of bed each morning, pause, stop your thoughts and consciously dial inward. Think of what you are grateful for. – List 2-3 reasons you are grateful.

2. Before getting out of bed each morning, think about your Life's Purpose, why life is meaningful to you.

3. Two times today pause, consciously turn inward for five to eight minutes connecting to your thoughts to your heart. In doing

so you will be developing your self awareness by checking your energy level. Do you have peace or tension in your heart?

4. What level of peace or tension do you have on a scale of 1-10 – 1 being low and 10 being high?

5. Get up and move, walk away from what you are doing. Distracting your mind by doing something completely different helps your mind sooth from any stress. Or talk to someone, perhaps saying to them "Hello _(name)_, how is your day?"

6. At the end of your night put distractions away (work, social media, tv, pets, phone, news, computer) for at least 30 minutes before going to bed.

7. Reflect on the level of peace or tension in your heart. – What is your level now and your reason how come?

Having self awareness of what you think about and how you consciously engage in your day will encourage you, keeping your mind clearer with focus, helping you in living and leading a flourishing life.

Blessings to being empathetic with joy, because giving comfort to yourself, and others, with feelings of pleasure and happiness builds energy towards having a heart at peace,
- Sara

Date: Day: Time:

PAUSE

Prepare | **A**cknowledge | **U**nderstand | **S**elf-Control | **E**ngage

---

Prepare

Read your Daily Drive

The Committed Way of Being, CWB

Circle the word 'Be' and circle how you are invited to 'Be' for today. *Example: **Daily Drive: Day One** (Be Humble)*

Conscious Awareness of Feeling, CAF

Circle the word 'with' and circle how you are invited to 'feel' for today. *Example: **Daily Drive: Day One** (with Love)*

The Reason 'How Come'

Draw a box around the word 'Because'.
Underline the words within the written Reason given for the day that stand out to you. *Example: **Daily Drive: Day One** Because*

*one of **the best opportunities to manage negative thoughts is** by expressing gratitude.*

Pause (Selah): Consciously connect within, being self-aware in attuning to your body's energy.

What tone are you currently sensing within your heart?

Circle: Peace | No Peace | Neutral | No Tension | Tension

Acknowledge

> ### PRAY
> *"Lord, thank you for today, and thank you for placing your Holy Spirit within me helping me have a heart of peace in managing my thoughts, feelings, words, and actions."*
>
> *God, strengthen me with power through Your Spirit in my inner being.*
> **- Ephesians 3:16**

Understanding

Reflect

- Consciously disconnect from any outlying distractions.

- Connect inward to your heart where the Holy Spirit resides.

- Connect your heart with your head, what is your head telling you about your heart:

_____

_____

- Identify or name the emotion(s) you are feeling:
(5 Core Emotions: 1. Sadness 2. Anger 3. Fear 4. Shame 5. Joy)

_____

Fill in the blanks:

Even Though I am feeling _____ it may cause tension within my heart and within my being, I am okay, God is with me.

I have every right to feel _____ it is not bad, it is normal, and God gives me the strength, endurance, and courage, to guard my heart with peace. I will get through this in time with His help.

Self-Control

Action Steps

Write or draw out your answer(s) to the question(s) from the
Daily Drive today:

Write out your responses for each Drive's Action Step below, on
index cards, or in a notebook:

_____

_____

_____

_____

_____

_____

Engage

1 2 3 4 5

Self-Awareness

On a scale of 1-5, rate yourself on how well you consciously and competently fulfilled the committed way of being, CWB, and conscious awareness of feeling, CAF, for the day and then write down your reason for how come, Because, you rated yourself how you rated yourself.

_____

_____

Close

Write 1-2 things you are taking away from the today's Daily Drive:

_____

_____

Write 1-2 things you can acknowledge yourself for from doing the today's Daily Drive:

_____

_____

Celebrate

- Say out loud:
  "I am thankful to God for my pursuing a heart of peace in living a flourishing life!"
- With a slight smile on one corner or both corners of your face.

'Living well is both a discipline and an art.'
- Sarah Young

AS WE HAVE *opportunity*,
LET US DO GOOD TO EVERYONE.

– GALATIANS 6:10

SOCIAL WELLBEING
Managing what you think, feel, say, and do

> *"A pessimist sees the difficulty in every opportunity; an optimist sees the opportunity in every difficulty."*
> - Sir Winston Churchill
>
> *And my God will supply every need of yours according to his riches in glory in Christ Jesus.*
> - Philippians 4:19

Today, perhaps, think about this:
Be teachable with peace because, ultimately, I cannot expect others to make me feel more secure, loved, and protected, only God can meet the deepest needs of my heart. Learning how to release control

gives my conscious mind freedom and gives my heart peace.

Gallup defines Social Wellbeing as having strong relationships and love in your life, the second of the five essential elements in living a flourishing life.

Action Steps:

(Write or draw answers under Action Steps in Self Control section of your journal.)

1. Write your name and write the names of 2-3 others within your social circles of your family, work, or community.

2. Next to each name, make a list of 2-3 specific ways you appreciate and value each person.

3. Keep this list in front of you and reread often.

4. Pause, Think and Reflect. Imagine seeing the person doing what you appreciate about them, then thank the Lord for their place in your life.

Examples:

My Name: Sara

Names of others within my family, work, or social circle:
Chris, Carol, Stephanie, Kim, Kirsten, and Catherine

I appreciate myself because **I am being intentional** in exercising three times a week, **one of my values is** self care.

I value having fun and _ **Stephanie** (write in someone in your social circle) makes me laugh, **I really appreciate** her sense humor.

Keep this list close to you because there will be a day(s) you may feel slighted by them (because this will happen). When this day arrives your heart and mind will be better prepared to appreciate and value them, rather than depreciate and devalue them, because your mind has been practicing appreciating and seeing them in a good light.

When feeling disrespected and devalued, about yourself or others, you can spiral into sadness, fear, anxiety or guilt. Even though you might have read the list many times before, reread it again. Seeing it written down helps your self awareness, keeping your mind consciously clearer and focused. You are teaching your heart and mind to have peace within your loving and supportive relationships, building energy and building healthy and happy relationships.

Blessings in being consciously competent, being teachable with peace, because thinking the best of others will help your heart shift from a heart at war to a heart at peace,
- Sara

Date: Day: Time:

PAUSE

Prepare | **A**cknowledge | **U**nderstand | **S**elf-Control | **E**ngage

---

Prepare

Read your Daily Drive
The Committed Way of Being, CWB
Circle the word 'Be' and circle how you are invited to 'Be' for today. *Example: Daily Drive: Day One* (Be Humble)

Conscious Awareness of Feeling, CAF
Circle the word 'with' and circle how you are invited to 'feel' for today. *Example: Daily Drive: Day One* (with Love)

The Reason 'How Come'
Draw a box around the word 'Because'.
Underline the words within the written Reason given for the day that stand out to you. *Example: Daily Drive: Day One* Because

*one of <u>**the best opportunities to manage negative thoughts is**</u> by <u>**expressing gratitude.**</u>*

Pause (Selah): Consciously connect within, being self-aware in attuning to your body's energy.

What tone are you currently sensing within your heart?
Circle: Peace | No Peace | Neutral | No Tension | Tension

Acknowledge

> PRAY
>
> *"Lord, thank you for today, and thank you for placing your Holy Spirit within me helping me have a heart of peace in managing my thoughts, feelings, words, and actions."*
>
> *God, strengthen me with power through Your Spirit in my inner being.*
> - Ephesians 3:16

Understanding

Reflect

- Consciously disconnect from any outlying distractions.

- Connect inward to your heart where the Holy Spirit resides.

- Connect your heart with your head, what is your head telling you about your heart:

_____

_____

- Identify or name the emotion(s) you are feeling:
(5 Core Emotions: 1. Sadness 2. Anger 3. Fear 4. Shame 5. Joy)

_____

Fill in the blanks:

Even Though I am feeling _____ it may cause tension within my heart and within my being, I am okay, God is with me.

I have every right to feel _____ it is not bad, it is normal, and God gives me the strength, endurance, and courage, to guard my heart with peace. I will get through this in time with His help.

Self-Control

Action Steps

Write or draw out your answer(s) to the question(s) from the
Daily Drive today:

Write out your responses for each Drive's Action Step below, on
index cards, or in a notebook:

_____

_____

_____

_____

_____

_____

Engage

1 2 3 4 5

Self-Awareness

On a scale of 1-5, rate yourself on how well you consciously and competently fulfilled the committed way of being, CWB, and conscious awareness of feeling, CAF, for the day and then write down your reason for how come, Because, you rated yourself how you rated yourself.

_____

_____

Close

Write 1-2 things you are taking away from the today's Daily Drive:

_____

_____

Write 1-2 things you can acknowledge yourself for from doing the today's Daily Drive:

_____

_____

Celebrate

- Say out loud:
  "I am thankful to God for my pursuing a heart of peace in living a flourishing life!"
- With a slight smile on one corner or both corners of your face.

'Living well is both a discipline and an art.'
- Sarah Young

AS IN WATER FACE *reflects* FACE, SO THE *heart* OF MAN REFLECTS THE MAN.

– PROVERBS 27:19

FINANCIAL WELLBEING
Managing what you think, feel, say, and do

> *"The quality, not the longevity, of one's life, is what is important."*
> - Martin Luther King Jr.
>
> *Outdo one another in showing honor. Do not be slothful in zeal.*
> - Romans 12:10-11

Today, perhaps, think about this:
Be respectful with patience because, if I, or those whom I have strong relationships and love in my life, are out of work, in transition, or unable to work, refuse to work, do not enjoy their work, I will need to be more creative to stay positive, patient, and optimistic.

Gallup defines Financial Wellbeing as how you effectively manage your economic life; it is the third of the five essential elements in living a flourishing life. An optional and creative strategy for being respectful is Co-Validation – one of every person's basic needs is being perceived as competent.

• If you do not believe you are competent or hear someone else tell you that you are incompetent this thought can have an unhealthy impact on your wellbeing. By creating a negative thought, that you are not good enough, this negativity could decrease your ability in living a flourishing life.

• If you do not perceive others as competent and they hear you criticize rather than encourage, they may react negatively, possibly projecting onto themselves or others incompetence. This can have an unhealthy impact on their wellbeing, decreasing their ability in living a flourishing life.

Co-Validation can help
If you or others in your close relationship and social circles are not very good at giving an affirmation, perhaps both of you may not be good at having empathy, Co-Validation could help.

Examples:
You: "Natalie, even though you do not have the job of your dreams right now, I am so proud of you for how you are working hard and being patient."

You: "Even though I am not working in the job of my dreams right now, I am proud of myself, working hard, and being patient."

You: "Tony, what a bummer you lost your job, wow, is that tough. I believe in you and believe your hard work in pursuing other job opportunities will pay off."

You: "Even though I lost my job, I have been out of work before and eventually found another job. Being optimistic will help me cope until I find another job."

Action Step:
(Write or draw answers under Action Steps in Self Control section of your journal.)

1. Say out loud and list 1-2 positive character qualities about yourself and 1-2 about the other person.

2. Say out loud and list 1-2 positive competencies about yourself and 1-2 about the other person.

3. Now practice co-validating by sharing 1-2 of each of your listed qualities with each other, about them and about yourself, because positive words build energy along with healthy and happy relationships..

God believes you are kind and competent, He believes in you. He is with you and He cares about you. In and through Him you have strength.

Blessings in being respectful with patience, having a heart of peace,
- Sara

Date: Day: Time:

PAUSE

Prepare | **A**cknowledge | **U**nderstand | **S**elf-Control | **E**ngage

---

Prepare

Read your Daily Drive
The Committed Way of Being, CWB
Circle the word 'Be' and circle how you are invited to 'Be' for
today. *Example: Daily Drive: Day One* (Be Humble)

Conscious Awareness of Feeling, CAF
Circle the word 'with' and circle how you are invited to 'feel' for
today. *Example: Daily Drive: Day One* (with Love)

The Reason 'How Come'
Draw a box around the word 'Because'.
Underline the words within the written Reason given for the day
that stand out to you. *Example: Daily Drive: Day One* | Because |

one of *the best opportunities to manage negative thoughts is* by
expressing gratitude.

Pause (Selah): Consciously connect within, being self-aware in
attuning to your body's energy.

What tone are you currently sensing within your heart?

Circle: Peace | No Peace | Neutral | No Tension | Tension

Acknowledge

PRAY
"Lord, thank you for today, and thank you for placing your Holy Spirit within me helping me have a heart of peace in managing my thoughts, feelings, words, and actions."

God, strengthen me with power through Your Spirit in my inner being.
- Ephesians 3:16

Understanding

Reflect

• Consciously disconnect from any outlying distractions.

• Connect inward to your heart where the Holy Spirit resides.

• Connect your heart with your head, what is your head telling you about your heart:

_____

_____

• Identify or name the emotion(s) you are feeling:
(5 Core Emotions: 1. Sadness 2. Anger 3. Fear 4. Shame 5. Joy)

_____

Fill in the blanks:

Even Though I am feeling _____ it may cause tension within my heart and within my being, I am okay, God is with me.

I have every right to feel _____ it is not bad, it is normal, and God gives me the strength, endurance, and courage, to guard my heart with peace. I will get through this in time with His help.

Self-Control

Action Steps

Write or draw out your answer(s) to the question(s) from the
Daily Drive today:

Write out your responses for each Drive's Action Step below, on
index cards, or in a notebook:

_____

_____

_____

_____

_____

_____

_____

Engage

1 2 3 4 5

Self-Awareness

On a scale of 1-5, rate yourself on how well you consciously and competently fulfilled the committed way of being, CWB, and conscious awareness of feeling, CAF, for the day and then write down your reason for how come, Because, you rated yourself how you rated yourself.

_____

_____

Close

Write 1-2 things you are taking away from the today's Daily Drive:

_____

_____

Write 1-2 things you can acknowledge yourself for from doing the today's Daily Drive:

_____

_____

Celebrate

- Say out loud:
  "I am thankful to God for my pursuing a heart of peace in living a flourishing life!"
- With a slight smile on one corner or both corners of your face.

'Living well is both a discipline and an art.'
- Sarah Young

PREPARE YOUR MIND FOR *action*, BE CLEAR MINDED AND HAVE *self-control*.

– 1 PETER 1:13-15

PHYSICAL WELLBEING
Managing what you think, feel, say, and do

"Contentment is not the fulfillment of what you want, but the realization of how much you already have."
- ANONYMOUS

And on the seventh day, God finished his work that he had done, and he rested on the seventh day from all his work that he had done.
- Genesis 2:2

Today, perhaps, think about this:
Be peaceful with gentleness because, even though sleep is very important to our health, not everyone is able to get a good night's rest.

Gallup defines Physical Wellbeing as having good health and enough energy to get things done on a daily basis; the fourth of the five essential elements in living a flourishing life.

Getting a good night's sleep is like hitting a reset button, clearing stressors away from the day. Scientists are discovering that people learn and make connections more effectively when they are asleep than when awake.

• Consciously watch your patterns.
• What you eat and drink at night has an impact.
• What you think at night has an impact, slow down your thoughts.
• Have your final thoughts at night be ones that give you a sense of calm.
• Relax in the evening, taking deep breathes.
• Put away and distract your mind from your work and any electronic distraction, news, and social media.
• Slow down your night activities.
• If you sleep well and others do not, allow freedom in others taking short naps to help reduce their stress levels and irritations due to not sleeping well at night.
• 7-8 hours of sleep each night has optimal benefits

When people have a heightened sense of sadness, fear, anxiety, guilt, they can forget to breathe, or they take small short breathes - whether awake or asleep, preventing good sleep.

Action Steps:
(Write or draw answers under Action Steps in Self Control section of your journal.)

Your brain needs oxygen
1. Pause, consciously think and draw inward, take three deep breathes filling your brain with oxygen, and clearing your mind. Perhaps pray, thanking God for blessings in your life.

2. Reflect on what is making you sad, fearful, anxious, ashamed, or guilty.

3. Replace the image with one that is good, maybe a body of water, the blue sky, a garden, heaven, or perhaps a sunset.

4. Practicing these steps helps you to cope, deescalate, self soothe, and calm your mind.

Practice deep breathing throughout each day, holding each breath for five-eight seconds:
- Before getting out of bed
- Mid-morning
- Mid-afternoon
- Before sleeping when in bed

Blessings in being peaceful with gentleness, having a heart of peace,
- Sara

Date: *Day:*   *Time:*

PAUSE

Prepare | **A**cknowledge | **U**nderstand | **S**elf-Control | **E**ngage

---

Prepare

Read your Daily Drive
The Committed Way of Being, CWB
Circle the word 'Be' and circle how you are invited to 'Be' for today. *Example: Daily Drive: Day One (Be Humble)*

Conscious Awareness of Feeling, CAF
Circle the word 'with' and circle how you are invited to 'feel' for today. *Example: Daily Drive: Day One (with Love)*

The Reason 'How Come'
Draw a box around the word 'Because'.
Underline the words within the written Reason given for the day that stand out to you. *Example: Daily Drive: Day One* | Because |

one of __the best opportunities to manage negative thoughts is__ by __expressing gratitude__.

Pause (Selah): Consciously connect within, being self-aware in attuning to your body's energy.

What tone are you currently sensing within your heart?
Circle: Peace | No Peace | Neutral | No Tension | Tension

Acknowledge

PRAY
"Lord, thank you for today, and thank you for placing your Holy Spirit within me helping me have a heart of peace in managing my thoughts, feelings, words, and actions."

God, strengthen me with power through Your Spirit in my inner being.
- Ephesians 3:16

Understanding

Reflect
• Consciously disconnect from any outlying distractions.

• Connect inward to your heart where the Holy Spirit resides.

• Connect your heart with your head, what is your head telling you about your heart:

_____

_____

• Identify or name the emotion(s) you are feeling:
(5 Core Emotions: 1. Sadness 2. Anger 3. Fear 4. Shame 5. Joy)

_____

Fill in the blanks:

Even Though I am feeling _____ it may cause tension within my heart and within my being, I am okay, God is with me.

I have every right to feel _____ it is not bad, it is normal, and God gives me the strength, endurance, and courage, to guard my heart with peace. I will get through this in time with His help.

Self-Control

Action Steps

Write or draw out your answer(s) to the question(s) from the
Daily Drive today:

Write out your responses for each Drive's Action Step below, on
index cards, or in a notebook:

_____

_____

_____

_____

_____

_____

Engage

1 2 3 4 5

Self-Awareness

On a scale of 1-5, rate yourself on how well you consciously and competently fulfilled the committed way of being, CWB, and conscious awareness of feeling, CAF, for the day and then write down your reason for how come, Because, you rated yourself how you rated yourself.

_____

_____

Close

Write 1-2 things you are taking away from the today's Daily Drive:

_____

_____

Write 1-2 things you can acknowledge yourself for from doing the today's Daily Drive:

_____

_____

Celebrate

- Say out loud:
  "I am thankful to God for my pursuing a heart of peace in living a flourishing life!"
- With a slight smile on one corner or both corners of your face.

'Living well is both a discipline and an art.'
- Sarah Young

LOVE ONE ANOTHER WITH BROTHERLY *affection*. OUTDO ONE ANOTHER IN SHOWING HONOR. LET YOUR SPEECH ALWAYS BE *gracious*, SEASONED WITH SALT, SO THAT YOU MAY KNOW HOW YOU OUGHT TO ANSWER EACH PERSON.

– COLOSSIANS 4:6

COMMUNITY WELLBEING
Managing what you think, feel, say, and do

> *"Coming together is a beginning. Keeping together is progress. Working together is success."*
> - Henry Ford
>
> *As we have opportunity, let us do good to everyone.*
> - Galatians 6:10

Today, perhaps, think about this,

Be appreciative with goodness because, no matter where you live, you live in a community with others.

Gallup defines Community Wellbeing as the sense of engagement you have within the area where you live; the fifth of the five essential elements and living a flourishing life.

Jesus is a perfect example of spending time, talking and hanging out, with all sorts of people. He went throughout all the cities and villages, teaching and healing every disease and affliction. He took the time to invest in other's lives. His goodness was one reason people were drawn to Him. -Matthew 9:10-13, 35

Action step:
(Write or draw answers under Action Steps in Self Control section of your journal.)

Today, how would you answer the following questions, evaluating your level of community wellbeing:

• In what ways is my community a good fit for my personality?

• What does my community offer that is a good fit for my family?

• Who are some individuals within my community I appreciate and enjoy spending time with?

• What interests do I have that I participate in within the community I live?

Today share with 1-3 people within your community one reason you appreciate their place in your life.

Blessings to being appreciative with goodness, in having a heart of peace,
- Sara

Date: *Day:*   *Time:*

PAUSE

Prepare | **A**cknowledge | **U**nderstand | **S**elf-Control | **E**ngage

---

Prepare

Read your Daily Drive

The Committed Way of Being, CWB
Circle the word 'Be' and circle how you are invited to 'Be' for today. *Example: **Daily Drive: Day One** (Be Humble)*

Conscious Awareness of Feeling, CAF
Circle the word 'with' and circle how you are invited to 'feel' for today. *Example: **Daily Drive: Day One** (with Love)*

The Reason 'How Come'
Draw a box around the word 'Because'.
Underline the words within the written Reason given for the day that stand out to you. *Example: **Daily Drive: Day One** [Because]*

*one of **the best opportunities to manage negative thoughts is** by **express**ing **gratitude.***

Pause (Selah): Consciously connect within, being self-aware in attuning to your body's energy.

What tone are you currently sensing within your heart?

Circle: Peace | No Peace | Neutral | No Tension | Tension

Acknowledge

Understanding

Reflect

• Consciously disconnect from any outlying distractions.

• Connect inward to your heart where the Holy Spirit resides.

• Connect your heart with your head, what is your head telling you
about your heart:

_____

_____

• Identify or name the emotion(s) you are feeling:
(5 Core Emotions: 1. Sadness 2. Anger 3. Fear 4. Shame 5. Joy)

_____

Fill in the blanks:

Even Though I am feeling _____ it may cause tension within
my heart and within my being, I am okay, God is with me.
I have every right to feel _____ it is not bad, it is normal, and
God gives me the strength, endurance, and courage, to guard my
heart with peace. I will get through this in time with His help.

Self-Control

Action Steps

Write or draw out your answer(s) to the question(s) from the Daily Drive today:

Write out your responses for each Drive's Action Step below, on index cards, or in a notebook:

_____

_____

_____

_____

_____

_____

Engage

1 2 3 4 5

Self-Awareness

On a scale of 1-5, rate yourself on how well you consciously and competently fulfilled the committed way of being, CWB, and conscious awareness of feeling, CAF, for the day and then write down your reason for how come, Because, you rated yourself how you rated yourself.

_____

_____

Close

Write 1-2 things you are taking away from the today's Daily Drive:

_____

_____

Write 1-2 things you can acknowledge yourself for from doing the today's Daily Drive:

_____

_____

Celebrate

• Say out loud:
  "I am thankful to God for my pursuing a heart of peace in living a flourishing life!"
• With a slight smile on one corner or both corners of your face.

'Living well is both a discipline and an art.'
- Sarah Young

CAREER WELLBEING

Managing what you think, feel, say, and do

> *"If you do what you have always done, you'll get what you have always gotten."* - Tony Robbins
>
> *You shall love the Lord your God with all your heart and with all your soul and with all your mind and with all your strength.*
> - Mark 12:30

For today, perhaps, think about this:

Be committed with faithfulness because, understanding your purpose and creating a vision in living a flourishing life takes time, self-reflection, patience, and endurance.

These past six days we have talked about the 5 Essential Elements of your Wellbeing,

"The currency of a life that matters. They do not include every nuance of what's important in life, but they do represent five broad categories that are essential to most people."

–Tim Rath & Jim Harter

1. Career Wellbeing
How you occupy your time or simply liking what you do every day.

2. Social Wellbeing
Having strong relationships and love in your life.

3. Financial Wellbeing
Effectively managing your economic life.

4. Physical Wellbeing
Having good health and enough energy to get things done on a daily basis.

5. Community Wellbeing
The sense of engagement you have with the area where you live.

Sixty-six percent of people are doing well in at least one of these areas, seven percent are thriving in all five. Struggling in any domain, as most of us are, damages our wellbeing and wears on our daily life. Research shows that the single biggest threat to our own wellbeing is ourselves. Without giving it much thought, we allow our short-term decisions to override what's best for our long-term wellbeing.

'Jesus' examples encourage us: Do not forget my teaching, peace will be added to you. Let not faithfulness forsake you; write them on the tablet of your heart. Trust in the Lord with all your heart, and do not lean on your own understanding.'

–Proverbs 3:1-35

Action step:
(Write or draw answers under Action Steps in Self Control section of your journal.)

On a scale of 1-5 (1= Struggling and 5=Fulfilled) rate the first two questions:

1. How peaceful is your heart and mindset?

2. How peaceful would you like your heart and mind to be?

3. What can you do for your first step?

Regularly connecting and talking with someone who is supportive, knowledgeable, and caring is essential. Someone who can help remind you to be committed with faithfulness to your purpose, your values, and your goals will help you have a heart of peace, living and leading a flourishing life.

Blessings in being committed with faithfulness, in having a heart of peace,
- Sara

Date: *Day:*   *Time:*

PAUSE

<u>P</u>repare | <u>A</u>cknowledge | <u>U</u>nderstand | <u>S</u>elf-Control | <u>E</u>ngage

---

Prepare

Read your Daily Drive
The Committed Way of Being, CWB
Circle the word 'Be' and circle how you are invited to 'Be' for today. *Example: Daily Drive: Day One (Be Humble)*

Conscious Awareness of Feeling, CAF
Circle the word 'with' and circle how you are invited to 'feel' for today. *Example: Daily Drive: Day One (with Love)*

The Reason 'How Come'
Draw a box around the word 'Because'.
Underline the words within the written Reason given for the day that stand out to you. *Example: Daily Drive: Day One* Because

one of <u>the best opportunities to manage negative thoughts is</u> by <u>express</u>ing <u>gratitude</u>.

Pause (Selah): Consciously connect within, being self-aware in attuning to your body's energy.

What tone are you currently sensing within your heart?
Circle: Peace | No Peace | Neutral | No Tension | Tension

Acknowledge

PRAY

"Lord, thank you for today, and thank you for placing your Holy Spirit within me helping me have a heart of peace in managing my thoughts, feelings, words, and actions."

God, strengthen me with power through Your Spirit in my inner being.
- Ephesians 3:16

Understanding

Reflect

• Consciously disconnect from any outlying distractions.

• Connect inward to your heart where the Holy Spirit resides.

• Connect your heart with your head, what is your head telling you about your heart:

_____

_____

• Identify or name the emotion(s) you are feeling:
(5 Core Emotions: 1. Sadness 2. Anger 3. Fear 4. Shame 5. Joy)

_____

Fill in the blanks:

Even Though I am feeling _____ it may cause tension within my heart and within my being, I am okay, God is with me.

I have every right to feel _____ it is not bad, it is normal, and God gives me the strength, endurance, and courage, to guard my heart with peace. I will get through this in time with His help.

Self-Control

Action Steps

Write or draw out your answer(s) to the question(s) from the Daily Drive today:

Write out your responses for each Drive's Action Step below, on index cards, or in a notebook:

_____

_____

_____

_____

_____

_____

Engage

1 2 3 4 5

Self-Awareness

On a scale of 1-5, rate yourself on how well you consciously and competently fulfilled the committed way of being, CWB, and conscious awareness of feeling, CAF, for the day and then write down your reason for how come, Because, you rated yourself how you rated yourself.

_____

_____

Close

Write 1-2 things you are taking away from the today's Daily Drive:

_____

_____

Write 1-2 things you can acknowledge yourself for from doing the today's Daily Drive:

_____

_____

Celebrate

- Say out loud:
  "I am thankful to God for my pursuing a heart of peace in living a flourishing life!"
- With a slight smile on one corner or both corners of your face.

'Living well is both a discipline and an art.'
- Sarah Young

BE *strengthened* WITH ALL POWER ACCORDING TO HIS GLORIOUS MIGHT SO THAT YOU MAY HAVE GREAT ENDURANCE AND *patience*.

– COLOSSIANS 1:11

CAREER WELLBEING
Managing what you think, feel, say, and do

"Every single person has a story that will break your heart. And if you're paying attention, many people... have a story that will bring you to your knees. Nobody rides for free."
- Brené Brown

May grace and peace be multiplied to you, being born again with a living hope, guarded through faith for salvation, because you have been grieved by various trials. The testing of your faith is more precious than gold... gold perishes. Though your faith is tested by fire, may your faith result in praise, glory, and honor of the revelation of Jesus Christ. Even though you have not seen him, you love him & believe in him, obtaining the salvation of your souls.
- 1 Peter 1:2-9

Today, perhaps, think about this:

Be teachable with kindness because, how you manage your cortisol and adrenaline levels has a direct impact on your emotional, mental, physical, and spiritual health in living a flourishing life.

After 40 years of research, Dr. John Gottman, with the Gottman Institute, shares that every person has an Emotional Bank Account. A person wakes up each day with approximately 9% emotional space giving an opportunity to a high risk of misinterpretation and miscommunication within relationships, at work and at home.

The increase in your cortisone (stress hormone), blood pressure, and adrenaline, might easily happen when you least expect or want it to happen. It does not take much to use 6% of the 9% before going out the door in the morning which could increase your cortisol and adrenaline levels, causing heightened frustration and anxiety.

-1% Waking up late
-1% No morning quiet time
-1% Only 1 cup of coffee instead of 2
-1% Concerns about work, school, weight, sleep, family, friends, life
-1% Getting ready and out the door
-1% _____ (you fill in the blank)

Action Step:
(Write or draw answers under Action Steps in Self Control section of your journal.)

Increase Your Self Awareness

1. Learn your behavioral patterns, observe yourself.

2. Pause, pray, reflect on what you are grateful for before getting out of bed each morning which helps to build your Emotional Bank Account.

3. Guard your heart, mind, and spirit, from any thought or feeling that could potentially deplete your emotional bank account.

4. Notice what makes you easily frustrated or offended.

5. Do at least one thing today that you enjoy.

Blessings in being teachable with faithfulness, having a heart of peace,
- Sara

Date: *Day:*   *Time:*

PAUSE

Prepare | **A**cknowledge | **U**nderstand | **S**elf-Control | **E**ngage

Prepare

Read your Daily Drive

The Committed Way of Being, CWB

Circle the word 'Be' and circle how you are invited to 'Be' for today. *Example: Daily Drive: Day One* (*Be Humble*)

Conscious Awareness of Feeling, CAF

Circle the word 'with' and circle how you are invited to 'feel' for today. *Example: Daily Drive: Day One* (*with Love*)

The Reason 'How Come'

Draw a box around the word 'Because'.

Underline the words within the written Reason given for the day that stand out to you. *Example: Daily Drive: Day One* | *Because* |

one of __the best opportunities to manage negative thoughts is__ by __express__ing __gratitude.__

Pause (Selah): Consciously connect within, being self-aware in attuning to your body's energy.

What tone are you currently sensing within your heart?

Circle: Peace | No Peace | Neutral | No Tension | Tension

Acknowledge

PRAY
*"Lord, thank you for today, and thank you for placing your
Holy Spirit within me helping me have a heart of peace in
managing my thoughts, feelings, words, and actions."*

God, strengthen me with power through Your Spirit in my inner being.
- Ephesians 3:16

Understanding

Reflect

• Consciously disconnect from any outlying distractions.

• Connect inward to your heart where the Holy Spirit resides.

• Connect your heart with your head, what is your head telling you about your heart:

_____

_____

• Identify or name the emotion(s) you are feeling:
(5 Core Emotions: 1. Sadness 2. Anger 3. Fear 4. Shame 5. Joy)

_____

Fill in the blanks:

Even Though I am feeling _____ it may cause tension within my heart and within my being, I am okay, God is with me.

I have every right to feel _____ it is not bad, it is normal, and God gives me the strength, endurance, and courage, to guard my heart with peace. I will get through this in time with His help.

Self-Control

Action Steps

Write or draw out your answer(s) to the question(s) from the
Daily Drive today:

Write out your responses for each Drive's Action Step below, on
index cards, or in a notebook:

_____

_____

_____

_____

_____

_____

_____

Engage

1 2 3 4 5

Self-Awareness

On a scale of 1-5, rate yourself on how well you consciously and competently fulfilled the committed way of being, CWB, and conscious awareness of feeling, CAF, for the day and then write down your reason for how come, Because, you rated yourself how you rated yourself.

_____

_____

Close

Write 1-2 things you are taking away from the today's Daily Drive:

_____

_____

Write 1-2 things you can acknowledge yourself for from doing the today's Daily Drive:

_____

_____

Celebrate

- Say out loud:
  "I am thankful to God for my pursuing a heart of peace in living a flourishing life!"
- With a slight smile on one corner or both corners of your face.

'Living well is both a discipline and an art.'
- Sarah Young

GUARD YOUR HEART WITH *vigilance* FOR FROM IT FLOWS THE SPRINGS OF *life*.

– PROVERBS 4:23

SOCIAL WELLBEING
Managing what you think, feel, say, and do

"Know yourself. Don't accept your dog's admiration as conclusive evidence that you are wonderful."
- **Ann Landers**

Accept one another, just as Christ Jesus accepted you.
- **Romans 15:7**

Today, perhaps, think about this:
Be humble with joy because, each person's heart and life, is valuable and important.

An element of having a flourishing Social Wellbeing is when you are able to identify others in your life who share a similar mission in life, spending more time with them because they encourage growth..

Action Steps:
(Write or draw answers under Action Steps in Self Control section of your journal.)

1. Think about individuals who have been an influence in your life?

2. What do you admire about them?

3. How much time do you spend engaging with them?

4. How do their behaviors seem to align with your core values?

5. What steps can you take to spend more time with those who encourage your growth?

Blessings in being humble with joy, having a heart of peace,
- Sara

Date: *Day:*   *Time:*

PAUSE

<u>P</u>repare | <u>A</u>cknowledge | <u>U</u>nderstand | <u>S</u>elf-Control | <u>E</u>ngage

---

Prepare

Read your Daily Drive

The Committed Way of Being, CWB

Circle the word 'Be' and circle how you are invited to 'Be' for today. *Example: Daily Drive: Day One* (Be Humble)

Conscious Awareness of Feeling, CAF

Circle the word 'with' and circle how you are invited to 'feel' for today. *Example: Daily Drive: Day One* (with Love)

The Reason 'How Come'

Draw a box around the word 'Because'.
Underline the words within the written Reason given for the day that stand out to you. *Example: Daily Drive: Day One* | Because |

one of <u>**the best opportunities to manage negative thoughts is**</u> *by* <u>**expressing gratitude.**</u>

Pause (Selah): Consciously connect within, being self-aware in attuning to your body's energy.

What tone are you currently sensing within your heart?

Circle: Peace | No Peace | Neutral | No Tension | Tension

Acknowledge

PRAY
*"Lord, thank you for today, and thank you for placing your
Holy Spirit within me helping me have a heart of peace in
managing my thoughts, feelings, words, and actions."*

God, strengthen me with power through Your Spirit in my inner being.
- Ephesians 3:16

Understanding

Reflect

- Consciously disconnect from any outlying distractions.

- Connect inward to your heart where the Holy Spirit resides.

- Connect your heart with your head, what is your head telling you about your heart:

_____

_____

- Identify or name the emotion(s) you are feeling:
(5 Core Emotions: 1. Sadness 2. Anger 3. Fear 4. Shame 5. Joy)

_____

Fill in the blanks:

Even Though I am feeling _____ it may cause tension within my heart and within my being, I am okay, God is with me.

I have every right to feel _____ it is not bad, it is normal, and God gives me the strength, endurance, and courage, to guard my heart with peace. I will get through this in time with His help.

Self-Control

Action Steps

Write or draw out your answer(s) to the question(s) from the Daily Drive today:

Write out your responses for each Drive's Action Step below, on index cards, or in a notebook:

_____

_____

_____

_____

_____

_____

Engage

1 2 3 4 5

Self-Awareness

On a scale of 1-5, rate yourself on how well you consciously and competently fulfilled the committed way of being, CWB, and conscious awareness of feeling, CAF, for the day and then write down your reason for how come, Because, you rated yourself how you rated yourself.

_____

_____

Close

Write 1-2 things you are taking away from the today's Daily Drive:

_____

_____

Write 1-2 things you can acknowledge yourself for from doing the today's Daily Drive:

_____

_____

Celebrate

- Say out loud:
  "I am thankful to God for my pursuing a heart of peace in living a flourishing life!"
- With a slight smile on one corner or both corners of your face.

'Living well is both a discipline and an art.'
- Sarah Young

SOCIAL WELLBEING
Managing what you think, feel, say, and do

> *"Be the friend you wish you would see in the world (would like to have)"*
> - Gandhi
>
> *Peace be to you. The friends greet you. Greet the friends, each by name.*
> - 3 John 15

Today, perhaps, think of this:

Be strong with love because, many people seem to feel lonely and isolated, a smile goes a long way!

Are you between the ages of 23 and 38? Are you lonely? According to a new survey by YouGov, if you answer yes to the first question, you're much more likely to answer yes to the second.

YouGov surveyed 1,254 Americans over 18 about friendship and loneliness:
- 30% Millennials the most likely age cohort to say they felt lonely "often" or "always."
- 20% Gen-X said they felt lonely often or always
- 15% Baby Boomers gave those answers
- 22% Millennials were also the most likely to report having zero friends
- 27% Zero close friends
- 25% Zero acquaintances

Millennials hold the dubious distinction of being our nation's loneliest generation.

Gallop research shares each person should spend close to six hours daily socializing with friends, family, and colleagues, via; work, home, phone, e-mail, and other communication. Those you least expect might be feeling lonely and isolated.

The 80-20 rule happens within relationships too:
80% do not reach out, 20% do

Being intentional in refilling in your social wellbeing might mean putting yourself out there and taking a risk. Connecting can sometimes feel scary in risking rejection.

Action Steps:
(Write or draw answers under Action Steps in Self Control section of your journal.)

- Make someone's day by reaching out and connecting to 1-2 people, serving them and lifting them up. – Who can you reach out to?

- What can you say to them in an effort of showing love, building energy and building relationships?

Blessings in being strong with love, having a heart of peace and a smile,
                                        - Sara

Date: *Day:*   *Time:*

PAUSE

<u>P</u>repare | <u>A</u>cknowledge | <u>U</u>nderstand | <u>S</u>elf-Control | <u>E</u>ngage

---

Prepare

Read your Daily Drive

The Committed Way of Being, CWB

Circle the word 'Be' and circle how you are invited to 'Be' for today. *Example: **Daily Drive: Day One** (Be Humble)*

Conscious Awareness of Feeling, CAF

Circle the word 'with' and circle how you are invited to 'feel' for today. *Example: **Daily Drive: Day One** (with Love)*

The Reason 'How Come'

Draw a box around the word 'Because'.

Underline the words within the written Reason given for the day that stand out to you. *Example: **Daily Drive: Day One** | Because |*

*one of **the best opportunities to manage negative thoughts is** by expressing **gratitude**.*

Pause (Selah): Consciously connect within, being self-aware in attuning to your body's energy.

What tone are you currently sensing within your heart?

Circle: Peace | No Peace | Neutral | No Tension | Tension

Acknowledge

Understanding

Reflect

• Consciously disconnect from any outlying distractions.

• Connect inward to your heart where the Holy Spirit resides.

• Connect your heart with your head, what is your head telling you about your heart:

_____

_____

• Identify or name the emotion(s) you are feeling:

(5 Core Emotions: 1. Sadness 2. Anger 3. Fear 4. Shame 5. Joy)

_____

Fill in the blanks:

Even Though I am feeling _____ it may cause tension within my heart and within my being, I am okay, God is with me.

I have every right to feel _____ it is not bad, it is normal, and God gives me the strength, endurance, and courage, to guard my heart with peace. I will get through this in time with His help.

Self-Control

Action Steps

Write or draw out your answer(s) to the question(s) from the Daily Drive today:

Write out your responses for each Drive's Action Step below, on index cards, or in a notebook:

_____

_____

_____

_____

_____

_____

Engage

1 2 3 4 5

Self-Awareness

On a scale of 1-5, rate yourself on how well you consciously and competently fulfilled the committed way of being, CWB, and conscious awareness of feeling, CAF, for the day and then write down your reason for how come, Because, you rated yourself how you rated yourself.

Close

Write 1-2 things you are taking away from the today's Daily Drive:

Write 1-2 things you can acknowledge yourself for from doing the today's Daily Drive:

Celebrate

- Say out loud:
  "I am thankful to God for my pursuing a heart of peace in living a flourishing life!"
- With a slight smile on one corner or both corners of your face.

'Living well is both a discipline and an art.'
- Sarah Young

FINANCIAL WELLBEING
Managing what you think, feel, say, and do

> *"Half our life is spent trying to find something to do with the time we have rushed through life trying to save."*
> - Will Rogers
>
> *For where your treasure is, there your heart will also be.*
> - Luke 12:34

Today, perhaps, think of this:
Be teachable with kindness because, people with thriving financial wellbeing, buy experiences, and those experiences along with their memories, can last a lifetime.

Usually, one partner or person in the family is more spontaneous with activities and creating experiences that give freedom in spending money than the other partner. That is okay, this is normal.

1. If I am more naturally spontaneous and fun-loving, perhaps God united my partner and me together to help one of us loosen up helping to stay optimistic during financial twists and turns of life.

2. If I am more naturally disciplined, perhaps God united us together to help one of us stay focused and disciplined. This does not include nagging or being contemptuous. Support each other with your financial and organizational skills.

Getting out and about creating fun experiences can sometimes be challenging. Each person has their own ideas of fun and spending money, activities may vary.

Some creative and fun memory producing ideas:
• 'Ordering To Go' - Themed Dining In meals - burger and fries might be like eating at a horse ranch. Everyone wears jeans, a flannel shirt, a western hat and only eats with their hands, no silverware.

• Creating a staycation - State Fair or Carnival - make homemade cream puffs, crepes, deep-fried cheese curds, corn dogs, chili cheese dogs, smoothies, or homemade funnel cakes with fun games like clothes pin drop and ring toss.

• Watch the same movie at the same time while zooming with family or friends - Everyone makes and enjoys their favorite movie snacks and drinks.

• Plot a garden or draw out blueprints and work on a project together.

Action Step:
(Write or draw answers under Action Steps in Self Control section of your journal.)

1. Do at least one fun activity one day a week.
   -Research encourages spending two hours in the activity if possible.

2. Put away all distractions and enjoy your time together.

3. Hang out with just your family or someone within your close circle of friends, often.
   -This includes people of all ages and stages of life.

Consciously notice how your energy and relationships shift!

Blessings being teachable with kindness, having a heart of peace,
- Sara

Date: *Day:*   *Time:*

PAUSE

Prepare | **A**cknowledge | **U**nderstand | **S**elf-Control | **E**ngage

---

Prepare

Read your Daily Drive
The Committed Way of Being, CWB
   Circle the word 'Be' and circle how you are invited to 'Be' for today. *Example: Daily Drive: Day One (Be Humble)*

Conscious Awareness of Feeling, CAF
   Circle the word 'with' and circle how you are invited to 'feel' for today. *Example: Daily Drive: Day One (with Love)*

The Reason 'How Come'
   Draw a box around the word 'Because'.
   Underline the words within the written Reason given for the day that stand out to you. *Example: Daily Drive: Day One │Because│*

   one of **the best opportunities to manage negative thoughts is** by **express**ing **gratitude.**

Pause (Selah): Consciously connect within, being self-aware in attuning to your body's energy.

What tone are you currently sensing within your heart?
Circle: Peace | No Peace | Neutral | No Tension | Tension

Acknowledge

Understanding

Reflect

• Consciously disconnect from any outlying distractions.

• Connect inward to your heart where the Holy Spirit resides.

• Connect your heart with your head, what is your head telling you about your heart:

_____

_____

• Identify or name the emotion(s) you are feeling:
(5 Core Emotions: 1. Sadness 2. Anger 3. Fear 4. Shame 5. Joy)

_____

Fill in the blanks:

Even Though I am feeling _____ it may cause tension within my heart and within my being, I am okay, God is with me.

I have every right to feel _____ it is not bad, it is normal, and God gives me the strength, endurance, and courage, to guard my heart with peace. I will get through this in time with His help.

Self-Control

Action Steps

Write or draw out your answer(s) to the question(s) from the
Daily Drive today:

Write out your responses for each Drive's Action Step below, on
index cards, or in a notebook:

_____

_____

_____

_____

_____

_____

Engage

1 2 3 4 5

Self-Awareness

On a scale of 1-5, rate yourself on how well you consciously and competently fulfilled the committed way of being, CWB, and conscious awareness of feeling, CAF, for the day and then write down your reason for how come, Because, you rated yourself how you rated yourself.

_____

_____

Close

Write 1-2 things you are taking away from the today's Daily Drive:

_____

_____

Write 1-2 things you can acknowledge yourself for from doing the today's Daily Drive:

_____

_____

Celebrate

- Say out loud:
  "I am thankful to God for my pursuing a heart of peace in living a flourishing life!"
- With a slight smile on one corner or both corners of your face.

'Living well is both a discipline and an art.'
- Sarah Young

LIVE SELF-CONTROLLED, BE *strong* IN THE LORD AND IN THE STRENGTH OF HIS MIGHT....PUT ON THE *whole armor* OF GOD, QUICK TO HEAR, SLOW TO SPEAK, SLOW TO ANGER.

– TITUS 2:12, EPHESIANS 6:10-16

PHYSICAL WELLBEING
Managing what you think, feel, say, and do

> *"Procrastination is opportunity's natural assassin."*
> - Victor Kiam
>
> *I have calmed and quieted my soul.*
> – Psalm 131:2

Today, perhaps, think of this:
Be forgiving with self control because, regardless of the country in which one lives, what is hugely encouraging is the speed at which healthy lifestyle changes can improve even the most chronic conditions.

People with thriving Physical Wellbeing effectively manage their health.

Researchers studying type 2 diabetes found:
    • People on a healthier diet could significantly reduce glucose, triglycerides, and cholesterol.
    • Decreasing their use of prescription medications by 43% - in just 4 1/2 months.

Perhaps you might be gaining unwanted weight, sitting more than moving, or having fearful or anxious emotions? If you are not, great. If you are struggling with fear and anxiety, something you may like to know is that those emotions can slow down your digestive system causing you unintentional weight gain and various internal health problems.

A diet with the right balance of healthy food is shown to:
    1. Alter the expression of genes that cause inflammation and allergies in just five weeks.

    2. Eating healthier and exercising regularly increases a person's positivity throughout the day, sharpening their thinking.

    3. Set positive defaults when shopping for groceries, loading up on natural foods that are red, green, and blue.

Action Steps
(Write or draw answers under Action Steps in Self Control section of your journal.)

    1. What are 1-3 behaviors you would be willing to change?

    2. What pattern would you be willing to alter?

    3. What can you do to discipline yourself?

You can change. Your patterns can be broken. You can be disciplined. Choose to be forgiving, having empathy with kindness for others and yourself.

If you are struggling:
- Reach out
- Connect
- Talk it out
- Write your thoughts down instead of holding thoughts inside

It's okay! You are not alone!

Blessings in being forgiving and having self-control, having a heart of peace,
- Sara

Date: *Day:*   *Time:*

PAUSE

<u>P</u>repare | <u>A</u>cknowledge | <u>U</u>nderstand | <u>S</u>elf-Control | <u>E</u>ngage

---

Prepare

Read your Daily Drive

The Committed Way of Being, CWB

Circle the word 'Be' and circle how you are invited to 'Be' for today. *Example: Daily Drive: Day One (Be Humble)*

Conscious Awareness of Feeling, CAF

Circle the word 'with' and circle how you are invited to 'feel' for today. *Example: Daily Drive: Day One (with Love)*

The Reason 'How Come'

Draw a box around the word 'Because'.
Underline the words within the written Reason given for the day that stand out to you. *Example: Daily Drive: Day One* | Because |

one of <u>**the best opportunities to manage negative thoughts is**</u> by <u>**express**</u>ing <u>**gratitude**</u>.

Pause (Selah): Consciously connect within, being self-aware in attuning to your body's energy.

What tone are you currently sensing within your heart?

Circle: Peace | No Peace | Neutral | No Tension | Tension

Acknowledge

PRAY

"Lord, thank you for today, and thank you for placing your Holy Spirit within me helping me have a heart of peace in managing my thoughts, feelings, words, and actions."

God, strengthen me with power through Your Spirit in my inner being.
- Ephesians 3:16

Understanding

Reflect

• Consciously disconnect from any outlying distractions.

• Connect inward to your heart where the Holy Spirit resides.

• Connect your heart with your head, what is your head telling you about your heart:

_____

_____

• Identify or name the emotion(s) you are feeling:
(5 Core Emotions: 1. Sadness 2. Anger 3. Fear 4. Shame 5. Joy)

_____

Fill in the blanks:

Even Though I am feeling _____ it may cause tension within my heart and within my being, I am okay, God is with me.

I have every right to feel _____ it is not bad, it is normal, and God gives me the strength, endurance, and courage, to guard my heart with peace. I will get through this in time with His help.

Self-Control

Action Steps

Write or draw out your answer(s) to the question(s) from the Daily Drive today:

Write out your responses for each Drive's Action Step below, on index cards, or in a notebook:

_____

_____

_____

_____

_____

_____

_____

Engage

1 2 3 4 5

Self-Awareness

On a scale of 1-5, rate yourself on how well you consciously and competently fulfilled the committed way of being, CWB, and conscious awareness of feeling, CAF, for the day and then write down your reason for how come, Because, you rated yourself how you rated yourself.

Close

Write 1-2 things you are taking away from the today's Daily Drive:

Write 1-2 things you can acknowledge yourself for from doing the today's Daily Drive:

Celebrate

- Say out loud:
  "I am thankful to God for my pursuing a heart of peace in living a flourishing life!"
- With a slight smile on one corner or both corners of your face.

'Living well is both a discipline and an art.'
- Sarah Young

SARA THINGVOLD
– AUTHOR BIO –

THINGVOLD

SERVING SMARTER AT HOME AND WORK

 facebook.com/SaraThingvold

linkedin.com/in/sarathingvold

www.sarathingvold.com

sarathingvoldprofessional@gmail.com

Professionally...

Sara Thingvold began coaching and training others as a sophomore in high school, starting her own coaching business in 2009 when living in Stillwater, MN. She is passionate about partnering and encouraging others toward heart renewal and servant leadership. With Sara's deep understanding of human behavior and her fun spirit, she helps leaders lead at work and at home.

Sara holds the following credentials:
- ICF ACC – Certified Executive Coach
  o Mastery, MCLC, Narrative, and Wellbeing
- Triune Leadership Services Coach, Trainer, and Consultant
- Gottman Institute PsychoEducational Leader and Trainer
  o Seven Principles of Making Marriage Work
  o Bringing Baby Home
- Certified Prepare/Enrich Facilitator
- B.A. Psychology, University of Nebraska-Lincoln
- Her published articles can be found worldwide, some include:
  o My First Step is Not to Step
  o Servant Leaders Lead, At Work And Home

Personally...

Sara's heart lives with her family. She and her husband have been married for 27 years. She is a proud retired military officer's wife whose husband served 32 years in the Army National Guard, through two deployments. They have two wonderful young adult children and a lovely daughter-in-law.

She is a University of Nebraska - Lincoln graduate and Husker Volleyball player Alumni. She enjoys the outdoors, cooking with her husband and family, gardening, hiking, running, crafting, and various other activities and hobbies, especially exercising her mind, body, and spirit, being intentional about deepening her own wellbeing.

MORE INFO

Visit www.sarathingvold.com to learn more information about what Sara has to offer and to sign up and receive Sara's Leadership Wellbeing articles and updates of newly published Daily Drive books.

Feel free to contact Sara to discuss possibilities on how she can help you in your *Living A Flourishing Life* journey. Transforming your way of living life!

SARA ✝HINGVOLD

SERVING SMARTER AT WORK AND HOME

Made in the USA
Columbia, SC
19 February 2021